# COUNTING THE COST

*Cycle C Sermons for
Proper 13 Through Proper 22
Based on the Gospel Texts*

## George Reed, O.S.L.

CSS Publishing Company, Inc.
Lima, Ohio

COUNTING THE COST

FIRST EDITION
Copyright © 2015
by CSS Publishing Co., Inc.

Published by CSS Publishing Company, Inc., Lima, Ohio 45807. All rights reserved. No part of this publication may be reproduced in any manner whatsoever without the prior permission of the publisher, except in the case of brief quotations embodied in critical articles and reviews. Inquiries should be addressed to: CSS Publishing Company, Inc., Permissions Department, 5450 N. Dixie Highway, Lima, Ohio 45807.

Scripture quotations marked (NRSV) are from the New Revised Standard Version of the Bible. Copyright 1989 by the Division of Christian Education of the National Council of the Churches of Christ in the USA, Nashville, Thomas Nelson Publishers © 1989. Used by permission. All rights reserved.

---

**Library of Congress Cataloging-in-Publication Data**

Reed, George (George E.), 1948-
   Counting the cost : Cycle C sermons for proper 13 through proper 22 : based on the gospel texts / George Reed. -- First edition.
      pages cm
   ISBN 0-7880-2821-9 (alk. paper)
   1. Bible. Gospels--Sermons. 2. Sermons, American--21st century. 3. Pentecost season--Sermons. 4. Church year sermons. 5. Common lectionary (1992). Year C. I. Title.

   BS2555.54.R44  2014
   252'.64--dc23

                                            2014037541

---

For more information about CSS Publishing Company resources, visit our website at www.csspub.com, email us at csr@csspub.com, or call (800) 241-4056.

e-book
ISBN-13: 978-0-7880-2822-9
ISBN-10: 0-7880-2822-7

ISBN-13: 978-0-7880-2821-2
ISBN-10: 0-7880-2821-9                                     PRINTED IN USA

*Dedicated to the memory of my mother,
Margaret June Overholser Reed,
who nurtured me in the faith and in the church.
Whatever passion resides in my work, I owe to her.*

OTHER TITLES WRITTEN BY GEORGE REED, O.S.L.:

**LECTIONARY WORSHIP AIDS, SERIES IX, CYCLE B**
0-7880-2669-0 / $29.95

**LECTIONARY WORSHIP AIDS, SERIES IX, CYCLE C**
0-7880-2674-4 / $28.95

**LECTIONARY WORSHIP AIDS, SERIES IX, CYCLE A**
0-7880-2702-6 / $27.95

**SERMONS ON THE GOSPEL READINGS, II, CYCLE B**
PENTECOST (MIDDLE THIRD)
0-7880-2370-5 / $24.95

OTHER TITLES FOR CYCLE C, GOSPEL TEXT
AVAILABLE THROUGH CSS ARE:

**GOD WITH SKIN ON**
ADVENT/CHRISTMAS/EPIPHANY
BY SUSAN R. ANDREWS

**CAN I GET SOME HELP OVER HERE?**
LENT/EASTER
BY R. ROBERT CUENI

**SPIRIT WORKS**
PENTECOST DAY THROUGH PROPER 12
BY ROBERT C. COCHRAN

**COUNTING THE COST**
PROPER 13 THROUGH PROPER 22
BY GEORGE REED, O.S.L.

**ORDINARY GRATITUDE**
PROPER 23 THROUGH CHRIST THE KING SUNDAY
BY MOLLY F. JAMES

# Table of Contents

Proper 13 / Pentecost 11 / Ordinary Time 18    7
Who's the Fool?
Luke 12:13-21

Proper 14 / Pentecost 12 / Ordinary Time 19    13
The Gift of the Kingdom
Luke 12:32-40

Proper 15 / Pentecost 13 / Ordinary Time 20    19
Know Jesus — No Peace
Luke 12:49-56

Proper 16 / Pentecost 14 / Ordinary Time 21    25
Freeing Those in Bondage
Luke 13:10-17

Proper 17 / Pentecost 15 / Ordinary Time 22    31
A Poor Banquet
Luke 14:1, 7-14

Proper 18 / Pentecost 16 / Ordinary Time 23    37
Counting the Cost
Luke 14:25-33

Proper 19 / Pentecost 17 / Ordinary Time 24    43
Joy as Our Hallmark
Luke 15:1-10

Proper 20 / Pentecost 18 / Ordinary Time 25    49
A Shrewd Christian?
Luke 16:1-13

**Proper 21 / Pentecost 19 / Ordinary Time 26**   55
   Worse Than It Sounds
   Luke 16:19-31

**Proper 22 / Pentecost 20 / Ordinary Time 27**   61
   Worthless Slaves
   Luke 17:5-10

## Proper 13 / Pentecost 11 / Ordinary Time 18
## Luke 12:13-21

*Someone in the crowd said to him, "Teacher, tell my brother to divide the family inheritance with me." But he said to him, "Friend, who set me to be a judge or arbitrator over you?" And he said to them, "Take care! Be on your guard against all kinds of greed; for one's life does not consist in the abundance of possessions." Then he told them a parable: "The land of a rich man produced abundantly. And he thought to himself, 'What should I do, for I have no place to store my crops?' Then he said, 'I will do this: I will pull down my barns and build larger ones, and there I will store all my grain and my goods. And I will say to my soul, "Soul, you have ample goods laid up for many years; relax, eat, drink, be merry." ' But God said to him, 'You fool! This very night your life is being demanded of you. And the things you have prepared, whose will they be?' So it is with those who store up treasures for themselves but are not rich toward God."*

Proper 13
Pentecost 11
Ordinary Time 18
Luke 12:13-21

# Who's the Fool?

This parable is often referred to as the parable of the rich fool and has been used to make any number of homiletical points. Some of them have even been relevant to the story! I have heard many a sermon preached on the "eat, drink, and make merry" portion of the scripture. We were warned about the dangers of having a good time. This was taken as a warning against what used to be called a "libertine lifestyle." But Jesus liked to party and have a good banquet. He made wine for the wedding feast and by his own admission was called a glutton and a drunkard because he enjoyed a good meal and wine. So let's stay away from this kind of interpretation of Jesus' parable.

Other times I have heard sermons which were based on those "who store up treasures for themselves but are not rich toward God" with the basic message that it is okay to be rich as long as we are good church members. After all, didn't Jesus say that? This is the same Jesus who told us we could not serve God and wealth. We must make our choice between the two. We can't serve two masters. We must also remember that in Jesus' day, agriculture was a subsistence economy. One did not get rich by working more hours and taking better care of the crops. If one was really diligent, one could hope to be able to feed the family and pay the Roman tax with maybe enough to give to the temple as well. That was really making it in Jesus' day for the honest farmer.

Those who were rich either inherited it or they became rich because they managed to get someone in their debt and then foreclosed on their land when they couldn't pay. To be rich, to have a super abundance of grain that required long-term storage was a certain sign that the wealth had been gathered on the backs and lives of others. One did not accumulate that amount of material goods while heeding the messages of justice or mercy. What Jesus is pointing out is the danger of greed, the danger of putting things ahead of God and ahead of people.

Most of us probably feel that while we are not perfect, we certainly would not put wealth before God. We are not idolaters who worship a golden calf. We would not steal land from people and deprive them of their ability to provide for themselves and their family. Or would we? Do we? One does not need to read very much from the Hebrew prophets to understand that God is very much interested in the plight of the poor and the underprivileged. God takes it personally when the poor are used for the gain of others. Jesus makes the point even clearer for those of us who might have missed it in the prophetic literature. He tells the story of the sorting of the sheep and the goats and explicitly states that the way we treat those in need is the way that we are treating him.

So if God self-identifies with the poor, how are we doing in the way we treat the poor and, therefore, God? Most of us probably don't think of ourselves as being very wealthy. We may be doing okay or we may even admit that we are "comfortable" in our lifestyle but few of us think of ourselves as wealthy. For those of us who live in America that feeling comes primarily from being surrounded by wealth. We are not surprised when we see anyone above the age of twelve carrying a cell phone. And it is probably a smart phone, so they basically have a handheld computer with them. Except in large cities, families have multiple cars and teenagers are often driving new, expensive automobiles. Jeans and sneakers that cost over $100 are not that rare. A family gathered around the one and only television in the house is nearly unheard of anymore.

Yet by global standards, if we have a place to live, any means of transportation, and do not eat the same basic thing for every meal, we are considered among the wealthy. We are so spoiled in this country by the incredible wealth that we do not understand just how much we have. But it is not our fault we were born here. We had nothing to do with our place of birth and we did not choose our parents, after all. And we are not tyrants. We are good people. Aren't we?

We try to do what is right. We vote according to what we see as the best options being offered to us. We support our local congregation and we give to charities beyond the church. We don't intend to do harm to folks, poor or otherwise. But the question Jesus brings to us is whether or not we see *him* when we look at those around us. Would we make the same decisions if we knew that Jesus was being effected by what we say and do?

Would we buy things made in sweatshops if we knew Jesus was working there? Would we be content to believe that it is okay because he is making more than he could if the shop wasn't there? Or would we want to know a little more about the working conditions? Is the place safe? Are there expectations of hours worked or goods produced that are beyond what we would tolerate from our employer? Are threats and manipulations causing him to work in ways that seriously compromise his health? In a global economy it is difficult to answer all these questions. It takes time and effort to make sure we are not supporting those who would treat our Savior so harshly. It takes time and effort to care. Is Jesus worth it? Or don't we really believe what he so plainly taught about being present in the persons of need?

There are few of us who would not agree that our welfare system is broken. Yet there are even fewer of us who are willing to do the work of really trying to understand the problem and coming up with ways to fix it other than depriving people of the benefits without understanding the need. We are accustomed to having a minimum wage and a set work week in this country but we forget that when Henry Ford came up with the idea and started these practices that it was a generous wage and reasonable hours that allowed his workers to take care of their families. What he really was offering was a livable wage and a livable work schedule. With only a few rare exceptions we are unwilling to even begin a discussion about a livable wage. Rather, we talk about the need for people to get off welfare and go to work but when people enter the work force at the minimum wage, they cannot earn a living working forty hours, or sixty, or many times, even eighty hours a week! And those hours usually come from working multiple, part-time jobs without benefits.

Now none of the solutions to these questions are easy to come up with. Especially when we take into account that Jesus the Christ is being affected by our decisions. We will not all agree on what solutions are best. But if together we address these issues with Jesus in mind and we trust one another to be seeking what is best for him, we can begin to make progress and we can make our Savior glad.

## Proper 14 / Pentecost 12 / Ordinary Time 19
## Luke 12:32-40

*Do not be afraid, little flock, for it is your Father's good pleasure to give you the kingdom. Sell your possessions, and give alms. Make purses for yourselves that do not wear out, an unfailing treasure in heaven, where no thief comes near and no moth destroys. For where your treasure is, there your heart will be also. "Be dressed for action and have your lamps lit; be like those who are waiting for their master to return from the wedding banquet, so that they may open the door for him as soon as he comes and knocks. Blessed are those slaves whom the master finds alert when he comes; truly I tell you, he will fasten his belt and have them sit down to eat, and he will come and serve them. If he comes during the middle of the night, or near dawn, and finds them so, blessed are those slaves. But know this: if the owner of the house had known at what hour the thief was coming, he would not have let his house be broken into. You also must be ready, for the Son of Man is coming at an unexpected hour."*

PROPER 14
PENTECOST 12
ORDINARY TIME 19
LUKE 12:32-40

# THE GIFT OF THE KINGDOM

Don't you just love gifts? I'm not talking about those hokey email scams where someone wants to give you $3.5 million if you will just send them all your private, financial information. I'm talking about real gifts whether they are wrapped up in ribbons or wrapped up in hugs. I don't know about you but I love gifts. Jesus is telling us that God has a gift for us: the kingdom. This is not a gift that comes out of obligation but is given with God's "good pleasure."

And it is a surprise gift, as well. Sometimes gifts surprise us because we didn't expect a gift at all but we get one, anyway. Other gifts surprise us because we were not expecting this particular gift. But there is another kind of surprise present where we keep discovering new things about the gift as time goes by. This is the kind of gift that Jesus tells us God is offering us.

That first surprise comes immediately after the announcement that we are receiving a gift. Jesus tells us to sell all that we have and help those who are in need. He tells us that there are two kinds of purses. There are those that wear out and whose contents can be destroyed or stolen, and there are those that last and cannot be lost. Jesus says that those in the realm of God carry the latter kind of purse. What kind of a gift has been given to us? Isn't a gift supposed to be a good thing that adds to what we have? Why then does this gift seem to take things away from us? What kind of a kingdom does God run, anyway?

Jesus doesn't leave us in the dark for long. He tells us that where we place our treasure, we will find our hearts. Whether we think of it as treasure, wealth, or just "our stuff." Jesus is aware that the things in our lives have a way of becoming the center of our lives. We usually don't mean for things to happen this way but the more we concentrate on something, the more important it becomes to us. The things that start out on the periphery of our lives have a way of working themselves onto center stage. We start looking after our retirement investments because that is the prudent thing to do and the next thing we know, we are checking the stock market reports on an hourly basis.

Jesus calls for us to sell what we have and give to those in need and that shocks us. We are taken back by such a demand and for good reason. Too often we have allowed the "stuff" of our lives to move too close to the center of our existence. We have given it too much power to determine our sense of worth. We begin to think of ourselves and others based on belongings and wealth instead of resting in our status as God's children. We are pulled into a world of superficial judgment, envy, and greed. There always seems to be someone who has more than we do and we begin to lust after the things others have. All of this leads to a world where things rule and people and relationships take the backseat. This is not the kingdom that God calls us into. We need that shock to get us to take a look at what we are doing to ourselves and to others.

One of the best ways we can begin to see where our treasure and our heart are located is to look at our checkbook. Where do we spend most of our money? What is it we spend our hard earned money on month after month? Far too many of us spend too much of our resources paying off debt on things that are long gone or for entertainment that has long been forgotten. Does our spending reflect what we want to value in life?

Another place to look is at our calendar. Where do we spend our time? Of course, for most of us, large portions of our day are set for us as we work or attend school or take care of children. But what about the rest of the time? Are we as careful about our devotional time and attending worship as we are about watching sports? What does our calendar say about our priorities?

Then after we take a look at these things, let's invite God to take a look at them with us. Bring your Bible and your devotional guides to prayer time if you want but bring your checkbook and calendar as well! Open them up before God and ask to see what is in them as God sees. This is not a time to rationalize to God or ourselves why we do what we do. This is a time to be honest with God and ourselves about what we do. And about what we should be doing. If those two don't coincide then we need to see what we can change and how we can change it.

Change is not easy and it sometimes takes a long time to get things the way they need to be. If we start rearranging our monetary priorities, the debt we have already piled up isn't going to just go away. We are going to have to deal with it. The commitments of our time that we have already made will still be there and we will have to work out the changes. But if we are serious about our discipleship then we are going to have to make sure that our treasures lead our hearts to Jesus and not to the mall.

God's gift to us is a big surprise and a wondrous gift. It calls us back to the reality of who we were created to be so that we can live out of that reality instead of the fantasy of material wealth. We are offered a place in God's realm where we matter just because we do. God has said that we are precious and that makes it so. When we quit trying to earn our place in God's world and just accept it as God's gift, then we can begin to really live. We can know wholeness and joy that no one and nothing can ever take away.

## Proper 15 / Pentecost 13 / Ordinary Time 20
## Luke 12:49-56

*I came to bring fire to the earth, and how I wish it were already kindled! I have a baptism with which to be baptized, and what stress I am under until it is completed! Do you think that I have come to bring peace to the earth? No, I tell you, but rather division! From now on five in one household will be divided, three against two and two against three; they will be divided: father against son and son against father, mother against daughter and daughter against mother, mother-in-law against her daughter-in-law and daughter-in-law against mother-in-law. He also said to the crowds, "When you see a cloud rising in the west, you immediately say, 'It is going to rain'; and so it happens. And when you see the south wind blowing, you say, 'There will be scorching heat'; and it happens. You hypocrites! You know how to interpret the appearance of earth and sky, but why do you not know how to interpret the present time?"*

PROPER 15
PENTECOST 13
ORDINARY TIME 20
LUKE 12:49-56

# KNOW JESUS — NO PEACE

How can we understand it when Jesus, the Prince of Peace, says, "Do you think that I have come to bring peace to the earth? No, I tell you, but rather division!"? What do we make of Jesus proclaiming that households will be divided because of him; that parents and children will be at odds? While some of the wits around us have used the pun of Know Jesus — Know Peace; No Jesus — No Peace, it seems that Jesus would have said Know Jesus — No Peace.

Jesus was aware of those around him who resisted the Roman occupation with violence and murder. He would have also known people who were willing to do anything to get along with the Romans. And, I am sure, there must have been those who just tried their best to ignore all this political talk and maneuvering and wanted to just get on with their lives. While Jesus seems to never sanction the use of force and violence, he also did not embrace either of the other ways to find peace. For Jesus there could be no peace without justice and mercy.

Jesus' whole life can be seen as a parable about what it means to stand up to oppression. It didn't matter to Jesus if the oppression was political, financial, or religious and often it was all three rolled into one. He could have spent his life wandering the hills of Galilee teaching and healing. He could have stayed away from the temple authorities and the Roman occupation forces. Or he even could have stayed with Mary and Joseph taking care of daily business. But that was not what he chose to do. Against all advice of family and friends, he turned his face to Jerusalem and went to face the oppressors.

Jesus didn't take an army with him but he went to call out the temple and Roman authorities for what they were: oppressors of the poor and needy. The Roman lash was terrible but no more destructive than the Roman tax. In the face of this oppression, the temple authorities did nothing to ease their own demands for the tithe. Instead of being the ones who spoke up for the poor, they added their own load to the burden the poor were forced to carry.

The *Pax Romana*, the Roman Peace, was based on brutal violence. If a disturbance breaks out among a group of people the way the Romans kept peace was to quickly and decisively put an end to the trouble. The only question was whether it was better to kill them all then or herd them up and crucify them later. Was it better to make the crowd cower with swift violence or better to let them see the trouble makers suffer slowly? Jesus knew that this peace was not really peace. It was violent hatred that did not count people as being of value. The way for the temple authorities to achieve peace was to cooperate with the Romans so that the temple trade was not disturbed and they could still receive the sacrifices, gifts, and tithes of the people. Jesus would confront both parties with the strongest weapon of all: truth. He presented himself to them and all could see them for what they truly were.

So why do we, Jesus' disciples, find it so hard to take a stand for what we believe in? The violence is all around us with school shootings coming so often that we have to identify which one we are talking about. The victims and perpetrators of acts of violence are getting younger and younger. Random shootings happen so often we have a special term for them, calling them drive-bys, and they are as common as the drive-thru windows at the fast food chains. Movies, television, and video games are full of the most graphic violence. Somehow we don't see how it is creating a culture of violence, and so we remain silent. And our children die around us.

There are those who say there are not enough studies to convince them that violence on TV and in video games produces a culture of violence but by the time the researchers have studied the effects of hours of daily violence on young people over ten year's time, it will be too late. You couldn't find a more effective way to brainwash someone than to get them to play games constantly that reward them for a certain behavior. That is what we are subjecting our children to in the most graphic, realistic forms.

At the very least, we need to insert some balance into the lives of the young people who have been entrusted to our care by God. We need to let them hear us state our belief in a God of love and a Savior who turned his back on violence as a means of solving problems. We need to stop worrying about whether or not our children like us as friends and see to it that they respect us as adults. This should be done not by being mean and oppressive to them but by spending time with them and talking with them about the really important issues in life. We need to take a stand.

Jesus still calls his disciples to follow, sometimes, right to Jerusalem and the very seat of power. Whatever authority brings oppression to those who are least able to defend themselves, Jesus marches to face them and he calls us to go with him. Whether it is religious folk sitting in judgment on others or government officials loading unfair tax burdens on the poor, it is still oppression. Whether it is government officials drawing large salaries and having wonderful healthcare while denying it to others or religious folks saying how much God loves them and hates others, it is still oppression.

Whatever form it takes, Jesus will be at the forefront leading the march to stand against such abuse and oppression.

Jesus calls us to take our place, to choose our side. He knows that not everyone will choose wisely. There will be those who choose, for whatever reason, to side with the oppressors. But decisions must be made. Stands must be taken. Peace that ignores oppression is no peace at all.

## Proper 16 / Pentecost 14 / Ordinary Time 21
## Luke 13:10-17

*Now he was teaching in one of the synagogues on the sabbath. And just then there appeared a woman with a spirit that had crippled her for eighteen years. She was bent over and was quite unable to stand up straight. When Jesus saw her, he called her over and said, "Woman, you are set free from your ailment." When he laid his hands on her, immediately she stood up straight and began praising God. But the leader of the synagogue, indignant because Jesus had cured on the sabbath, kept saying to the crowd, "There are six days on which work ought to be done; come on those days and be cured, and not on the sabbath day." But the Lord answered him and said, "You hypocrites! Does not each of you on the sabbath untie his ox or his donkey from the manger, and lead it away to give it water? And ought not this woman, a daughter of Abraham whom Satan bound for eighteen long years, be set free from this bondage on the sabbath day?" When he said this, all his opponents were put to shame; and the entire crowd was rejoicing at all the wonderful things that he was doing.*

PROPER 16
PENTECOST 14
ORDINARY TIME 21
LUKE 13:10-17

# FREEING THOSE IN BONDAGE

The story of Jesus healing the woman with a crippling spirit while he was teaching in the synagogue one sabbath is about a lot more than what is appropriate to do on the sabbath. It is a window into the mindset of Jesus about ministry.

The first thing we notice in this story is that Jesus is teaching in the synagogue on the sabbath. This sounds like such a traditional means of worship and teaching to us. Many Christians have adopted the term sabbath for Sunday, the Lord's Day, and talking about Jesus being in worship on the sabbath makes us feel more connected to him and better about what we do on Sunday mornings. It seems like a really big affirmation that it is okay for us to stick to our traditional ways of doing things. If it was okay for Jesus, it ought to be okay for us!

There are some problems with this type of reading of the story, however. The first is historical. We know that worship changed in Israel. From the Abrahamic covenant with its very unique ritual and its renewal in the visit of the three strangers to the time when Moses called the entire people to participate in the covenant-making and to join in the sacrifices that took place in the tabernacle that traveled with them. With David and Solomon the worship centered in a specific place, Jerusalem, and then an even more specific place with the building of the temple there. When the temple was destroyed and the people went into exile they wondered, "How can we sing the Lord's song in a strange land?" Those who returned to Jerusalem for the rebuilding of the temple were excited by the finding of the Torah. The new temple wasn't as grand as the last but at least there was a place to sacrifice. But many did not return and Jerusalem was not the center of their world anymore.

Jesus was participating in the faith community in the way that made sense and was open to the people at the time. The people were poor and oppressed. To put together enough resources to feed the family and be able to plant another crop was to be successful. There were no extra funds for a family pilgrimage to the temple in Jerusalem. They could not afford to go annually for the Passover and most would never be able to make the trip. The answer for them was to offer sacrifices of obedience instead of animals. They studied the Torah and they tried to follow it as best they could knowing that the conditions of their lives made much of it unattainable. If Jesus' presence in the synagogue signified anything it was his openness to honoring God in whatever way one was able.

The second problem with reading this story as a stamp of approval on our traditional way of doing things is clearly presented when Jesus healed the woman with the crippling spirit on the sabbath. If you thought Jesus was giving the thumbs up to tradition over all, then think again. The religious leaders were appalled when Jesus healed the woman on the day of rest. This was not the way things were to be done. In fact, this was in direct contradiction to what God's word says! No work on the sabbath. It is clearly stated and Jesus had violated this basic tenet of Judaism.

But Jesus had an answer to this criticism. He spoke first of all of the very humane practice that devout Jews followed on watering and feeding the livestock on the sabbath. They were God's creatures and they were not to be mistreated on the sabbath any more than on any other day. And if that was true for the livestock it was certainly true for the creatures made in the image of God. It made no sense to treat animals humanely and humans with cruelty. And it was cruelty, Jesus asserted, to not free this woman who had been bound by her affliction for all those years.

It was not tradition that mattered most we learned from Jesus, although he often participated in it. It was meeting the needs of God's creatures and God's people. Whether it was in the needs of the people to worship in a different way or whether it was in the needs of the people to be set free from their bondage, it was and is the need of the people that matters most to Jesus. When the traditions met these or, at the very least did not add to those needs, then Jesus was content to live within them. But when they did not meet the needs of the people he is willing to go outside the tradition and when the tradition blocked the meeting of the peoples' needs, he was very adamant on putting the people above the tradition.

Perhaps if we could re-frame our discussions about change in terms of the compassion of Christ and the needs of the people instead of in terms of tradition, we could at least begin to listen to one another. If we listened with the ears of Jesus to a person who has suffered great abuse from the hands of their own father, perhaps we could understand better how difficult it is to call God our Father. It may be a dear term to me that I learned as a child and one that makes me glad but perhaps it is blocking this needy one from realizing the grace of our God. Maybe I could, at least for a time, use another term for God in worship and hold the term Father for my personal devotions, not because the pastor or the worship committee has placed those terms in the bulletin but because of the compassion of Christ. We see this compassion in the story of healing on the sabbath. Scripture does offer many alternatives.

If I looked at other people in terms of their needs instead of in terms of my standards, perhaps I would be less prone to judgment and more prone to service and ministry. A youth group on a mission trip were helping to repair a leaking roof for a family. While the youth worked, the father of the family they were helping sat on the porch in his rocker. He offered no help for the project even though it was to help him and his family. When the youth were talking about it later some of them wondered why he didn't help. After all, even if he was poor he was still healthy, he could have joined in the project. What is wrong with poor people? One member of the youth group spoke up and said, "The problem isn't that he is broke. The problem is that he is broken."

This teenager looked on the man with the compassion of Christ and saw someone for whom hope was no longer possible. Instead of seeing a lazy man who wouldn't help himself or his family, she saw a man that life had cruelly crushed so that he couldn't even see the use of fixing a hole in the roof of his house. If there is any help for that man and his family beyond just repairing the roof, it will have to come out of the kind of compassion and insight this youth group member displayed. Telling him he is lazy and no good will not help. Giving him hope is the only thing that can help. Telling him and showing him that God loves him and he is important is the only start to his healing. Seeing the need and moving to meet it is the way of Christ. It is the way of setting free those who have been in bondage.

## Proper 17 / Pentecost 15 / Ordinary Time 22
## Luke 14:1, 7-14

*On one occasion when Jesus was going to the house of a leader of the Pharisees to eat a meal on the sabbath, they were watching him closely.... When he noticed how the guests chose the places of honor, he told them a parable. "When you are invited by someone to a wedding banquet, do not sit down at the place of honor, in case someone more distinguished than you has been invited by your host; and the host who invited both of you may come and say to you, 'Give this person your place,' and then in disgrace you would start to take the lowest place. But when you are invited, go and sit down at the lowest place, so that when your host comes, he may say to you, 'Friend, move up higher'; then you will be honored in the presence of all who sit at the table with you. For all who exalt themselves will be humbled, and those who humble themselves will be exalted." He said also to the one who had invited him, "When you give a luncheon or a dinner, do not invite your friends or your brothers or your relatives or rich neighbors, in case they may invite you in return, and you would be repaid. But when you give a banquet, invite the poor, the crippled, the lame, and the blind. And you will be blessed, because they cannot repay you, for you will be repaid at the resurrection of the righteous."*

PROPER 17
PENTECOST 15
ORDINARY TIME 22
LUKE 14:1, 7-14

# A POOR BANQUET

At first glance the advice Jesus gave on taking a spot at a banquet seemed to just be common sense. Society was very regimented and social standing was incredibly important. One who was more "important" than another person would receive a better seat at a banquet. Class A celebrities got to sit closer to the host than class B celebrities. Even if the celebrity status was based on the number of sheep in their flock.

So when Jesus told folks they should take a seat of inferior status so they would not get bumped down and embarrassed, it sounded like just smart, social maneuvering. No one wants to end up red-faced because they are being demoted publicly. And who wouldn't want to be singled out by the host and brought up to a higher seat? That Jesus is a pretty shrewd operator, it would seem.

The truth is Jesus is more shrewd than we may give him credit for in this teaching. In a society where people are looking to place themselves above others, Jesus is getting them to think about who they are below instead of who they are above. Now, instead of saying, "I am better than this person so I can sit farther up front than they are sitting," they begin to say, "I might not be as cool as this person, I better sit behind them." What a difference in attitude Jesus is calling us to take.

And if the host is busy and most of us are not as important as we think we are, it is possible that even if we sit farther back than we need to sit, the host might not notice or have the time to move us. Or we may not be important enough for him to bother with us! So all we can conclude is that perhaps we were right in placing ourselves where we did. We really are not more important than that person. Whatever the case, it teaches us to approach the situation with a whole new attitude.

While our society is not structured quite like in Jesus' day, we still have our levels and think about people of higher and lower status. We might stand in line for hours to get an autograph of a famous baseball player, but we probably are not going to ask the kids playing in the empty lot down the street for their autograph! Nor are we going to be so anxious to get the autograph of the person on the minor league squad as we are to get one from someone in the majors.

We may notice what the person ahead of us in line buys at the supermarket if they are paying with food stamps but if the person has the cash, we wouldn't think to criticize their purchases. I love the story that tells of the farmer who having taken his load of wheat to the grain exchange stopped by the Cadillac dealership to buy a new car. The salesperson was new and didn't know the farmer. He felt he could not waste his time on someone so poorly dressed. He did not know the farmer had the money with him to pay cash for the car. The salesperson lost the sale, the commission, and the opportunity to sell another car to the man later. In large and small ways, we are often making assumptions about the worth of a person. And often we are making the assumption that we are better than they.

Today, as in Jesus' day, people often think in terms of reciprocity. If you give me a gift at Christmas then I have to give you one. If you hold the door open for me then I need to hold the next door open for you. At one level it is just a matter of being polite but what happens when the other person doesn't respond in a manner that we think is appropriate? What happens when we hold the door for them and they just walk on and let the next door fly shut in our face? What do we think of the person when we have spent a lot of time and money on picking out just the right gift for them at Christmas and they give us nothing in return? Jesus teaches us how to avoid the upset of not receiving in return: give to those you know can't return the favor.

When we think about it, this is the type of giving that God does. There is nothing we can really give God because God has everything. Even our lives belong to God so God does not give to us in order to receive something back. God gives because God loves us and because we have needs. Jesus teaches us that God is not one who decides to stop blessing us because we haven't said thank you often enough or because we haven't put enough money in the offering plate at church. God gives because it is the nature of the God of love to give. God gives because God loves us and wants us to be whole and joyful in our lives.

Since we are created in the image of God, it is part of our nature to be givers who do not have strings attached to the gifts. As God's people we are not fully who we were created to be when we think in terms of gift reciprocity. We must be the kind of gift givers that God is if we truly want to be happy. Unfortunately most of us know the frustration of feeling hurt and angry because someone has slighted us by either not giving us a gift or giving us a gift that is "less valuable" than the one we gave them. We know how it eats at us destroying our sense of happiness and destroying our relationship with that person. What does it get us besides being angry and depressed? Absolutely nothing!

So Jesus teaches us to take another route. Look at gift giving and party throwing as an opportunity to reach out to those who are in need. Some congregations have begun to hold Thanksgiving dinner and Christmas dinner for anyone in the community who wants to come. There is no cost for it and, most importantly, it is actually held on Thanksgiving and Christmas Day. They don't give people a dinner *like* a holiday meal. They give them a real meal on the real holiday. Giving for these people is more important than being with family. They know that not only for those who are poor but for those who are alone, having a nice meal with people on the holiday is the most wondrous gift of all. They know they are not alone. They know that nothing is expected of them except that they enjoy the meal. They know they are loved by these people and that, therefore, it just might be possible that God loves them as well.

## Proper 18 / Pentecost 16 / Ordinary Time 23
## Luke 14:25-33

*Now large crowds were traveling with him; and he turned and said to them, "Whoever comes to me and does not hate father and mother, wife and children, brothers and sisters, yes, and even life itself, cannot be my disciple. Whoever does not carry the cross and follow me cannot be my disciple. For which of you, intending to build a tower, does not first sit down and estimate the cost, to see whether he has enough to complete it? Otherwise, when he has laid a foundation and is not able to finish, all who see it will begin to ridicule him, saying, 'This fellow began to build and was not able to finish.' Or what king, going out to wage war against another king, will not sit down first and consider whether he is able with ten thousand to oppose the one who comes against him with twenty thousand? If he cannot, then, while the other is still far away, he sends a delegation and asks for the terms of peace. So therefore, none of you can become my disciple if you do not give up all your possessions."*

PROPER 18
PENTECOST 16
ORDINARY TIME 23
LUKE 14:25-33

# COUNTING THE COST

Jesus certainly cannot be accused of using a "soft sell" approach when it comes to calling folks to discipleship. While salespeople are taught to extol the good points, ignore the bad points, and wait until you have your customer hooked before you deliver the price to them, Jesus comes out with the price right up front. And it is steep. Jesus doesn't offer us a sign-and-drive option to follow him. He tells us this is going to be a costly adventure and we better be willing to ante up if we are going to join. The cost? Everything. Family, friends, comfort, and even our own lives are to be offered up for this chance to follow Jesus on the way into the reign of God. That certainly makes it easy for those of us in congregations and denominations of declining memberships! That should have them flocking to us in droves!

The problem for us is that we are too often focused on the organization and its needs. We don't have enough members to fill all the leadership spots and the choir numbers are way down. We have had to reduce the hours the secretary is in the church office and do away with the youth pastor because the budget just couldn't sustain them anymore. The building is in need of repair and we can't even keep up with the regular maintenance costs. All of these things are filling our minds while Jesus is focused on one thing and one thing only: the reign of God. Bringing the reign of God into the lives of people and into the life of the world is all that really matters.

Jesus understands that many things compete for our attention. There are lots of important things happening in our lives. Some of them may be destructive to us but most of them are good things. The problem isn't the things but the importance we put on them. Our priorities mis-order the events, people, and things in our lives and then we are in trouble. We put our jobs before our families and soon we find ourselves in divorce court and our children have become strangers to us. We become fixated on our physical appearance and abilities only to find that the steroids and weird diets have ruined our health. We decide we can be popular if we just do the things that someone tells us to do and find ourselves regretting our decisions as we carry a criminal record with us for the rest of our lives.

Priorities — we have to have them or we will find ourselves adrift in life without a real direction. But be careful because wrong priorities, even when they involve good things, can get us in a world of hurt. Jesus understands this and calls people to put God's reign first which is the only way we can then rightly judge where on the scale the rest of the things in our lives belong. It is good to love and respect your parents. It is a wonderful thing to be devoted to your spouse and children. Being good at your work and dedicated to what you do is fine. It is a whole lot more fun to have money than not. But let any of these goals rise up to proclaim themselves number one in your life and it can destroy you.

Parents are meant to nurture us and care for us as they guide us into adulthood. But parents are people and they are fallible. There are not only the emotionally crippled parents who abuse their children but there are parents who will not let go of their children so that they can take their place in society as adults. There are parents who think they can make the best choices for their children about career choices no matter how old the child is or how much the child despises the choice the parent makes. And there are wonderful parents who have the best of intentions and desires for their children but they suffer from that awful condition called "being human." As wonderful as parents can be, they can't be what we build our lives on.

All must be given up so that God and God's reign can become number one. As long as we hold tightly to other things we cannot make God first in our lives. We are just too prone to push family, wealth, job, or other things above God. It is only when we are willing to let go of them completely that we can put God first. When we have emptied our hands and offered them up in allegiance and prayer to God, then we can begin to deal with people as people and with objects as objects and not confuse them with being gods. When we have given them up and seen them for what they are, gifts from God, then we no longer see them as the ultimate objects of our lives.

When our lives are properly ordered with God and God's reign being number one then we are free to receive and enjoy the good gifts that God desires us to have. Then we can receive the gift of family and celebrate it in all its goodness and offer forgiveness in all its failures. Without the pressure to make it perfect, we can accept it for what it is. When we have let go of money as ultimate measure of our worth and placed God and God's love there, we can use the wealth, however large or small, that comes our way rejoicing that we have received it from God's generous hand. When we have learned to know our place in God's love then we don't have to worry about our place in the minds of those around us. If they think well of us and laud our accomplishments, that is nice. If they ignore us or think us lowly and untalented, it does not matter. We are God's and God loves us eternally and unconditionally. We are in a right relationship with God and nothing else matters.

This is what Jesus was getting at when he told us that if we seek after the kingdom of God, God's reign, first then everything else will fall into place. Once God and God's desire for creation are put first in our lives then we can sort out and reorder the rest as seems best to us. Whatever we turn our minds and hands to can become blessed if they are done to the glory of God and growth of God's realm.

Seek ye first the kingdom of God.

## Proper 19 / Pentecost 17 / Ordinary Time 24
## Luke 15:1-10

*Now all the tax collectors and sinners were coming near to listen to him. And the Pharisees and the scribes were grumbling and saying, "This fellow welcomes sinners and eats with them." So he told them this parable: "Which one of you, having a hundred sheep and losing one of them, does not leave the ninety-nine in the wilderness and go after the one that is lost until he finds it? When he has found it, he lays it on his shoulders and rejoices. And when he comes home, he calls together his friends and neighbors, saying to them, 'Rejoice with me, for I have found my sheep that was lost.' Just so, I tell you, there will be more joy in heaven over one sinner who repents than over ninety-nine righteous persons who need no repentance. Or what woman having ten silver coins, if she loses one of them, does not light a lamp, sweep the house, and search carefully until she finds it? When she has found it, she calls together her friends and neighbors, saying, 'Rejoice with me, for I have found the coin that I had lost.' Just so, I tell you, there is joy in the presence of the angels of God over one sinner who repents."*

Proper 19
Pentecost 17
Ordinary Time 24
Luke 15:1-10

# Joy as Our Hallmark

In the past the complaint by folks about Christianity was that it was too austere. No card playing, no dancing, no anything on Sunday except worship and quiet conversation. Then in the '60s the folk mass movement began and has blossomed after fifty years into the praise and worship movement. Now the complaint is that Christianity is mindlessly happy. Songs that have no real depth of meaning are sung over and over again. Nothing but 7/11 music is the comment: songs that only have seven words and are sung eleven times over. Where is the depth? Where is the meaning? And it is not just the outsiders complaining. Many of us in the church have participated in the famous *worship wars* in numerous congregations.

In the gospel reading for today we have Jesus responding to the criticism of the religious folks about his hanging out with folks of poor repute. There are three stories he tells and we have two of them today: the lost sheep and the lost coin parables. In all three the emphasis is on the joy at finding the lost. There are parties but we don't have a lot of details about the celebrations in the first two stories. We just know that the person who found the lost rejoiced with their friends over the finding.

Whether our personalities are boisterous and loud or quiet and reflective is not the issue. Whether we sit quietly in candlelight with soft organ music and the scent of incense wafting through the worship space or whether we are standing with hands waving over our heads with a band playing at full volume is not the hallmark of whether we are Christians doing Christian worship or not. No, our hallmark is that we are people of joy and that joy is based on the love of God who never gives up on us.

Joy is that deep quality of peace and contentment that comes from knowing that we are loved and nothing in heaven, on earth, or in hell can ever separate us from the love of God we have received through Jesus the Christ. How that joy gets expressed has more to do with our personalities and the personality of our congregation than it does with the quality or reality of our religious experience.

Sometimes joy does burst out in song and dance and sometimes joy sits quietly in the wondrous moment of peace. Our joy may be so strong that it seems we will burst if we don't tell everyone we see about it and sometimes it is so intense that it is beyond words and all we can do is sit quietly in awe and wonder as we contemplate the love of our God. It is not the expression that makes the joy true but it is the reality of God's presence, grace, and love that makes it real.

The question for us revolves around whether or not we are people of joy. It is not whether or not we are happy all the time because life does not lend itself to making us happy constantly. There are sad things that happen and we experience loss and grief on a regular basis. Sickness, death, job loss, financial reversals, relationships that do not work out, and many other things come our way and they are not happy times. That is the nature of our existence. But at a deeper level the nature of our existence is to be held in the grace and love of God that cannot be defeated by any of these circumstances. It is learning to say with Saint Paul that we are content no matter what is happening.

We can be quiet in worship because we are deep in contemplation or because we are so spiritually dead that nothing touches us. We can be exuberant with song and dance in worship because we are filled with the Spirit or because we are in a manic phase fueled by sugar and caffeine. But joy comes only from the reality of love. We experience it when we are loved by other people but we experience it at its deepest when it is based on the love of God.

For many of us, if not all of us, the most effective conduit for God's love is through another human. We are made as composite beings. That wondrous story of creation where God forms a human creature out of the earth and then breathes into it God's own breath, life, and Spirit speaks volumes about who we are. We are mortal and based on the earth. We are made of the same components as the earth on which we live. But we are more than that because there resides within us the very life breath of God. We are mortal and divine. We are made in the image of God. As Christians we proclaim that we are the very Body of Christ. We are God's presence in physical form in this world.

Being both human and divine we find that often for us to understand and receive God's presence and love, it needs to come to us through human interaction. God tried pillars of fire and of cloud, thunder, and smoke, and deep silence to share God's love with us. Finally he gave us Jesus as the Christ who brought God's presence to us. Apparently God was pleased with this method because he gave to the world the church which was created by taking human beings and endowing them with God's own Spirit. We were made Christians, little Christs, who as disciples of Jesus endeavor to share God's love and grace with others.

In the parables of the lost sheep and lost coin, the finders called together their friends to celebrate and rejoice. God's love and redemption are meant to be shared. It is in the human contact and giving of the love we have received from God that God's joy, and ours, is made complete. God did not create us to be alone. God created us for communion with the divine and God created us for communion with each other. When we combine these two elements and share God's love with others, joy is the result. As we see God's love made manifest in the lives of others it makes our joy more complete. As they receive God's love through our care and compassion, their joy is brought to fruition. Joy is the peace and contentment of knowing we are loved unconditionally. It is the hallmark of who we are as God's people and as Jesus' disciples.

# Proper 20 / Pentecost 18 / Ordinary Time 25
## Luke 16:1-13

*Then Jesus said to the disciples, "There was a rich man who had a manager, and charges were brought to him that this man was squandering his property. So he summoned him and said to him, 'What is this that I hear about you? Give me an accounting of your management, because you cannot be my manager any longer.' Then the manager said to himself, 'What will I do, now that my master is taking the position away from me? I am not strong enough to dig, and I am ashamed to beg. I have decided what to do so that, when I am dismissed as manager, people may welcome me into their homes.' So, summoning his master's debtors one by one, he asked the first, 'How much do you owe my master?' He answered, 'A hundred jugs of olive oil.' He said to him, 'Take your bill, sit down quickly, and make it fifty.' Then he asked another, 'And how much do you owe?' He replied, 'A hundred containers of wheat.' He said to him, 'Take your bill and make it eighty.' And his master commended the dishonest manager because he had acted shrewdly; for the children of this age are more shrewd in dealing with their own generation than are the children of light. And I tell you, make friends for yourselves by means of dishonest wealth so that when it is gone, they may welcome you into the eternal homes. Whoever is faithful in a very little is faithful also in much; and whoever is dishonest in a very little is dishonest also in much. If then you have not been faithful with the dishonest wealth, who will entrust to you the true riches? And if you have not been faithful with what belongs to another, who will give you what is your own? No slave can serve two masters; for a slave will either hate the one and love the other, or be devoted to the one and despise the other. You cannot serve God and wealth."*

Proper 20
Pentecost 18
Ordinary Time 25
Luke 16:1-13

# A Shrewd Christian?

For many the term "shrewd Christian" is an oxymoron as these two terms just seem to be so opposite in their minds. But in the parable of the unjust steward Jesus calls on his disciples to become as shrewd in doing good as others are in doing evil. According to Webster's dictionary shrewd means "keen-witted, clever, or sharp in practical matters." We have often used the word in its secondary sense of cunning and in a context where one has used their intellect to take advantage of a person or a situation in an unethical way. Jesus calls us to be as shrewd in ethical ways as others are in unethical ways.

The manager in Jesus' story is a shrewd fellow in the worst sense of the word. He has misused his master's resources. We don't know the exact nature of the crime but he has obviously been converting his master's resources for his own use. He has been placed in charge of wealth to manage it for the owner and, instead, has been skimming for himself. When he gets caught he does not repent or change his ways. Instead, he ups the ante and goes all out on the course he has begun.

Calling those who were in debt to his master he proposed to change their bills so that they would owe less. In this way he hoped to make friends of these folks so that he could be taken care of after he was dismissed. As he himself noted he was too weak to dig and too proud to beg. He also entangled them in his dishonesty so that he could use their complicity in his dishonesty against them to make sure they would take care of him.

The folks who are in debt were very shrewd in a dishonest sense as well. They saw an opportunity to relieve themselves of debt and increase their bottom line. We don't know what arguments they used to justify themselves, if any, but they didn't hesitate to take advantage of the situation. When Jesus told a story to get across a point, he used things that his audience could relate to, things that they understood. He didn't seem to need to explain this story. They would have been no more surprised that someone was embezzling from the company than we are when we hear those news stories today.

The real surprise is the response of the owner. He commended his dishonest manager for his shrewdness. Yes, he had been taken advantage of but, we suspect, he had done the same in *his* dealings with others. He understood what *chutzpah* it took to embark on a course of more dishonesty and thievery when one had already been caught in the act.

Jesus then went on to make his first point. It was a shame that those who were dishonest were more shrewd than those who were honest. If the children of light were as sharp-witted as the children of this generation then we would be making more progress in bringing in the kingdom. God created us with minds that can reason and think things out and we should use those God-given powers for good. As Galileo Galilei stated, "I do not feel obliged to believe that the same God who has endowed us with sense, reason, and intellect has intended us to forgo their use." Jesus and Galileo seem to be on the same page here. If God didn't want us to think, God would not have created us with that power.

The Episcopal church in America ran an ad some time ago that contained the line, "You don't have to leave your brain at the door" and a United Church of Christ congregation has a cartoon heart and brain holding hands with the line, "hearts and brains welcome here." It really shouldn't be a stretch for the church to welcome intellect. The number of colleges and universities that have been founded by the church is vast. Some of the deepest and hardest to follow papers have been offered up on theology. Yet when it comes to conducting our affairs in the world, we can be very sloppy and shortsighted. Jesus tells us clearly that is not the way for us to conduct our business. We should be as sharp-witted as anyone when it comes to the business side of the church.

And yet Jesus is very clear that we are do this in the midst of being disciples. We are the folks who know that justice and mercy are our calling. We can only find our way in the world with those who exhibit unethical shrewdness if our shrewdness is wrapped tightly in the love and compassion of God. Money should be used well as money but it should never be used in a way when it becomes a weapon that wounds others. We should invest wisely but we should not invest in companies that are involved in actions that harm people. It is another place where not having our priorities in place can be disastrous.

We can only base our lives on one point. We can plant ourselves firmly on the solid bedrock of God or we can place ourselves on the shifting sands of wealth. We can't be divided in our commitment. But once we have firmly established that God is the touchstone of all our decisions, then we are free to be clear-thinking, logical, and — yes — shrewd in our dealings. When in humility before God we embrace justice and mercy as our guidelines, then we can be as keen-witted as the world.

The trick is to avoid the temptation to allow our shrewdness to take us away from the priorities God calls us to. We can never forget who it is that we serve. We cannot hold God in first place on Sunday morning and place material gain, even for the church, above God's way during the week. There is no dual citizenship in God's realm. We are either living under the rules of God or we are living under the influence of evil. That is not to say that we don't make mistakes or that we don't choose poorly. It is not to say that we do not miss the mark and fail miserably sometimes as God's people but no one can live in both realms at the same time. An old adage in the spiritual literature of the church acknowledges that there is no neutral gear for the Christian. We either move forward or backward — and we can't do both at once.

So let us embrace the intellect and reasoning ability that God has given us and use it with all its power for God.

## Proper 21 / Pentecost 19 / Ordinary Time 26
## Luke 16:19-31

*There was a rich man who was dressed in purple and fine linen and who feasted sumptuously every day. And at his gate lay a poor man named Lazarus, covered with sores, who longed to satisfy his hunger with what fell from the rich man's table; even the dogs would come and lick his sores. The poor man died and was carried away by the angels to be with Abraham. The rich man also died and was buried. In Hades, where he was being tormented, he looked up and saw Abraham far away with Lazarus by his side. He called out, "Father Abraham, have mercy on me, and send Lazarus to dip the tip of his finger in water and cool my tongue; for I am in agony in these flames." But Abraham said, "Child, remember that during your lifetime you received your good things, and Lazarus in like manner evil things; but now he is comforted here, and you are in agony. Besides all this, between you and us a great chasm has been fixed, so that those who might want to pass from here to you cannot do so, and no one can cross from there to us." He said, "Then, father, I beg you to send him to my father's house — for I have five brothers — that he may warn them, so that they will not also come into this place of torment." Abraham replied, "They have Moses and the prophets; they should listen to them." He said, "No, father Abraham; but if someone goes to them from the dead, they will repent." He said to him, "If they do not listen to Moses and the prophets, neither will they be convinced even if someone rises from the dead."*

PROPER 21
PENTECOST 19
ORDINARY TIME 26
LUKE 16:19-31

# WORSE THAN IT SOUNDS

The story of the rich man, often called Dives, and Lazarus is a heartrending tale of suffering on the part of the poor man and indifference on the part of the rich one. If that was all the story was about it would be dreadful enough but it also shows us the horrors of society when it is divided into classes. We see this clearly in the attitude of the rich man.

While the rich man is comfortably situated in his luxurious home there is a beggar outside his gates who is starving to death. He is a miserable wretch and the rich man could not have missed seeing him. Even today where we go from our homes directly into our garages, get in our cars, and drive away from our homes we would see if someone was lying at the end of our driveway. There is no reason to suspect that this man had darkened glass on his camel. He knew the man was there but he didn't care because the man was not worth caring about.

He may have thought him a nuisance but he didn't see him as another human being in need. It was not just that the man had no compassion or care for others. Later in the story he is very concerned about his own brothers. Those who were like him, he cared for. Those who are beneath him were not worth bothering with. He was just a worthless old beggar who was getting what he deserved. If he was a good person God would take care of him. If he was an industrious person who worked hard, he would have resources to take care of himself. If he was a likeable guy then his family or friends would take care of him.

I am sure the rich man saw nothing wrong with being rich. He was a hard worker and he contributed to the local synagogue. He probably even went to temple at Passover. God had blessed him with abundance because he was such a good fellow. He certainly felt that he had received what he deserved.

I wonder about Lazarus. Did he feel the same way? It is not out of the question. Often when people are down on their luck, get laid off because the company is down-sizing, or are stricken with illness, they feel as if they deserve it. Often they don't express it quite so directly but we hear someone say, "It happened for a reason." And most of the time the reason is known by God who has sent this hardship on them for their own good. Because of some lack they have or some sin they have done, they feel they deserve to receive the hardship. We have no record of Lazarus rising up and going to the door and demanding food. We have no record that he even went to the door to beg. He just laid there. And the rich man let him lie and so did the community. Until finally Lazarus died at the rich man's gate and in time the rich man also died.

It would seem that equality had finally been achieved but that was not so. Lazarus was received into the arms of Father Abraham and the rich man was buried and found himself in torment. When the rich man asked Father Abraham about this he was told that while Lazarus suffered on earth and he had good things, the tables had been switched.

But listen to the rich man. Here he was looking up at Lazarus in the bosom of the eternal while he was being tormented and he asked Father Abraham to "send" Lazarus down to quench his thirst. Even in this situation, he still sees Lazarus as beneath him, as someone who should be taking care of him. The man who never lifted a finger to help the poor beggar wanted that beggar to leave his place of comfort and go down and serve him! The arrogance never ends.

When Father Abraham explained that it was impossible for anyone "down there" to come up to them and that a gulf was fixed so that anyone "up here" who would want to could not go down, the rich man still saw Lazarus as the underling. He wanted Lazarus to be sent on an errand to warn the rich man's brothers about this place. "Well, you know, they have Moses and the prophets who have told them how to live and they should listen to them," Father Abraham said. "Oh, but if someone rose from the dead they would listen," he rejoined. But Father Abraham knew that if they were blind to the truth, it didn't matter what form it took. They would still be blind.

When we judge people and place them in categories we are beginning an incredibly fast descent down a slippery slope. When we see people who are suffering and do not see them as children of God — as our sisters and brothers — we are setting ourselves up for a very nasty fall. Jesus was very clear in telling us not to judge, not to condemn others. Don't set up standards and then decide that others have not met them. That was his message for us. We are called to be like our God who makes the sun shine on the good and the bad, who sends the rain on the just and unjust. It is that kind of unconditional love that we are often not able to grasp.

When Jesus went about his ministry he reached out to all. He went in to eat in the houses of tax collectors and sinners and he went in to eat in the houses of the religious leaders. Their reactions to him differed in many ways but Jesus was open to share God's love with them all. The only words of rebuke we ever hear from the lips of Jesus are directed against those who tried to shut others out from the grace and love of God.

Who do we see and who don't we see as children of God? Who do we have compassion for and who are we willing to believe that they are just getting what they deserve when they have bad things happen to them?

## Proper 22 / Pentecost 20 / Ordinary Time 27
## Luke 17:5-10

*The apostles said to the Lord, "Increase our faith!" The Lord replied, "If you had faith the size of a mustard seed, you could say to this mulberry tree, 'Be uprooted and planted in the sea,' and it would obey you. Who among you would say to your slave who has just come in from plowing or tending sheep in the field, 'Come here at once and take your place at the table'? Would you not rather say to him, 'Prepare supper for me, put on your apron and serve me while I eat and drink; later you may eat and drink'? Do you thank the slave for doing what was commanded? So you also, when you have done all that you were ordered to do, say, 'We are worthless slaves; we have done only what we ought to have done!'"*

PROPER 22
PENTECOST 20
ORDINARY TIME 27
LUKE 17:5-10

# WORTHLESS SLAVES

In the movie *Raiders of the Lost Ark* Indiana Jones has to choose which cup would have belonged to Jesus and been used at the Last Supper. There are dozens upon dozens to choose from and each seems more lavish than the next. He chooses the one which is the most simple and would most likely reflect the lifestyle of a simple carpenter. It is the correct choice. While there may be some problems with using this movie as a theology guide at this point it is right on. Jesus is the humble one who came to serve and not to be served.

In this gospel lesson we have a teaching from Jesus on the kind of attitude we need to assume as followers of the Christ. Jesus used a very simple story about a man who had come into his house after a hard day's work. Jesus offered a very humorous suggestion asking if we, as the master of the house, would have our slaves sit down while we fed them. The crowd listening to Jesus would have known the answer right away not because they owned slaves but because they were poor and served others and perhaps were even slaves themselves. No master is going to serve the slaves. He is going to expect them to take care of him and his needs and he isn't going to gush over their wonderful service and leave a large tip. They can expect nothing, not even a thank you.

Jesus says that this is the way we should look on our service that we render up to God. We should consider ourselves no more than slaves who are called to be obedient. When we do what we are suppose to do we should not pat ourselves on the back or expect God to pat us on the head and tell us how wonderful we are. We should, instead, respond, "We are worthless slaves; we have done only what we ought to have done" (v. 10). There is no talk of stars in our crowns or of the huge palace we will have in heaven. There is just the acknowledgment that we have done no more than was expected of us.

This is a difficult concept for most of us in the church to understand. In the Roman Catholic church there are many who have trouble with the behavior of Pope Francis. He is the only pope to take the name of Saint Francis of Assisi who lived such a humble life of poverty. He does not live in the fanciest part of Vatican City. He eats with others and eats the same food as they do. He seems to take seriously his title: chief servant of the people of God.

We often think that we are something special because we are Jesus' disciples. We do what is good and right so we must be better than others, right? Not according to Jesus. We have been called to love God with our entire being, our heart, soul, strength, and mind. Nothing less than this will do. Most of us feel how awesome the task set before us is and we know that we have not achieved this kind of devotion to our God. And yet, even if we do achieve it, we have done nothing extraordinary. No, we have only done what has been asked of us.

In the same way, we are asked to love others as we love ourselves. We are told to give the same careful consideration to the needs of others that we give to our own needs. Most of us are pretty clear that we have not attained this kind of holiness even before Jesus reminds us that he isn't talking about just our family and friends but about strangers and those we would consider our enemies. And if we should somehow manage to achieve such a goal, the angels of heaven may be surprised but they won't be falling down in awe and wonder of us. We have only done what has been asked of us and nothing more. We are just worthless slaves.

Some may conclude that God is a heartless, cruel master who doesn't deserve to be obeyed if this is the way things are. But we have to be careful here. Jesus does not say a word about the master's attitude. Jesus couches the conversation in terms of what we would do if we were the master and what we would expect of our slaves. The lesson Jesus gives us is about our attitude as servants of the most high and is not a theological treatise on God's nature. No matter how good we think we may be, we are to be humble and unassuming.

Reflect on Jesus' teaching about greatness in God's economy. It does not come from being the one who is served but by offering oneself as the servant of all. There is a quiet humility in Jesus and his teachings that is very powerful for it does not ask us to debase ourselves but, rather, to lift up the other person. The humility of Jesus has nothing to do with wearing hair shirts or inflicting pain upon our bodies. It consists in lifting up the lowly and not expecting any praise or reward for it. It is a humility based on compassion.

Humility is living in the truth of who we are and all of us are wonderfully gifted and terribly flawed. We are God's image and yet we are mired in the clay of the earth. From Saint Paul's declaration that he is the worst of sinners to John Wesley denying his achieving of perfection in this life (though he taught it could be achieved) to the confessions of Mother Teresa, we have examples of those who knew the truth of how to serve God in the way of Jesus. We are not above others. We are only servants who, at best, have done only what we were told to do.

When we can serve God and God's creatures with this kind of Christ Spirit, then we begin to participate in the joy of Jesus. In this humble attitude we are removed from trying to prove ourselves and to make ourselves worthy of God's love. In this attitude we can serve joyously knowing we are side-by-side with the Christ.

www.ingramcontent.com/pod-product-compliance
Lightning Source LLC
Chambersburg PA
CBHW072014060426
42446CB00043B/2549